Early Praise for *A RATTLE]*

"This delightful book turns tail on the human-centric view of the universe most of us unwittingly subscribe to. Narrated by a black rattlesnake and captivatingly illustrated by a fisheries biologist, *A RATTLER'S TALE* logs a year's worth of interactions between a human family and the Arizona wildlife that inhabit the environs of their mountain cabin. By good (and occasionally bad) example, the book teaches that all creatures have a place in the colorful tapestry of creation."

— **Cindy Yurth President of the Black Hat Humane Society**

"*A Rattler's Tale* is a wonderful set of short animal/human encounters that bring awareness of how we are so connected to our habitat and the animals that live in it, just out of sight (for the most part). A great read for adults and children alike and a stepping off point to start important conversations about how we treat the world around us. The rattler's narrative is informative, yet personal, and brings the reader into the viewpoint of an often-feared species."

— **Kay Bordwell, Grand Canyon Sierra Club Group Executive Committee for wildlife**

"This is a wonderful book about humans' relationship with nature, enhanced by delightful illustrations. As the coordinator for 20 years of the read aloud literacy programs, BookPALS and Sunshine Readers, I would endorse this book as a great read aloud for 3rd through 6th graders or even older. Each chapter can stand alone, but the quirky animal characters and especially the snake narrator who ties the whole thing together, will have the kids begging for "just one more chapter." There are excellent follow-up questions and projects at the end of the book so students can continue their investigation into the wonders of the natural world and their relation to it. It is time we ALL learned to appreciate and respect each other. *A RATTLER'S TALE* emphatically sends that message."

— **Ellen Dean, Literacy Advocate**
http://www.storylineonline.net

A RATTLER'S TALE

When Wild Animals Encounter Humans

Nancy Hicks Marshall

Illustrated by
Lauren Sarantopulos

Nugget Press
Phoenix, AZ

Nugget Press
4009 E Coolidge St
Phoenix, AZ 85018
www.NuggetPress.com

ISBN   978-0-9828259-0-7   print
ISBN   978-0-9828259-1-4   ebook

Interior and Cover design – Anita Jones, Another Jones Graphics
Illustrations - Lauren Sarantopulos

Publisher's Cataloging-In-Publication Data
(Prepared by The Donohue Group, Inc.)

Names: Marshall, Nancy Hicks, 1941- author. | Sarantopulos, Lauren, illustrator.
Title: A rattler's tale : when wild animals encounter humans / Nancy Hicks Marshall ; illustrated by Lauren Sarantopulos.
Description: Phoenix, AZ : Nugget Press, [2021] | Interest age level: 007-011. | Includes bibliographical references and index. | Summary: "With the national forest as a backdrop, one of its important creatures, the Arizona Black Rattlesnake narrates many short stories about the surprising and creative interaction between wild animals who call this place home and humans who are only visitors"--Provided by publisher.
Identifiers: ISBN 9780982825907 (print) | ISBN 9780982825914 (ebook)
Subjects: LCSH: Human-animal relationships--Anecdotes--Juvenile literature. | Wild animals--Anecdotes--Juvenile literature. | Animals and civilization--Anecdotes--Juvenile literature. | CYAC: Human-animal relationships--Anecdotes. | Wild animals--Anecdotes. | Animals and civilization--Anecdotes. | LCGFT: Anecdotes.
Classification: LCC QL85 .M37 2021 (print) | LCC QL85 (ebook) | DDC 590--dc23

Printed in the United States of America

For
Vance, Elias and Hilary
You lived it.

and for
Readers everywhere, Young and Old,
May you gain an even greater appreciation for
our wild animal brothers and sisters

TABLE OF CONTENTS

CAST OF CHARACTERS

The National Forest is our stage.

Here, in order of appearance, you will encounter:

※ One Arizona Black Rattlesnake (*crotalus cerberus*);

※ Mr. and Mrs. Red-Tailed Hawk (*búteo jamaicénsis*);

※ The Human being family (*homo sapiens*);

※ The Pet Dog (*canis familiaris*);

※ Rose, the Striped Skunk (*mephitis mephitis*);

※ Lonely Mr. Great-Tailed Grackle (*quíscalus májor*);

※ Harry the Hare, aka Jackrabbit (*Lepus californicus*), *not* a Jackalope

※ Junior, the Black Bear (*ursus Americanus*);

※ A Western Blue Bird mom and her chick (*siália mexicana*);

※ Blaze (the American Quarter Horse);

※ Rocky, the Common Raccoon (*procyon lotor*);

※ More field mice than I can count (*mus musculus*);

※ Twenty Javelina, aka collared peccary (*tayassu tajacu*);

※ The White-Tailed Deer family (*odocoileus Virginianus*);

※ One Mountain Lion (*puma concolor*)

※ Ramona Ringtail (*bassariscus astustus*), the Arizona State Mammal.

※ Other creatures of the wild, all an essential part of this habitat, may be present, but they are too numerous to mention. However, they provide essential background to these stories.

INTRODUCTION

Hello! Thanks for coming on this journey and letting me tell you some stories from my perspective. It's a wild adventure.

After all, it's not every day a snake gets to tell the story.

Here we are in the middle of the National Forest, which is home to many, many animals. Humans are usually only visitors. As I slither around on the ground, and into rocky crevices, I often see my fellow wild ones encounter those human visitors.

Let's start at the beginning.

I am an Arizona Black Rattlesnake. Unlike the diamondback rattler, who lives primarily in desert areas and has pale tan desert colors for camouflage, I am black (hence the name), with lovely rich white-, gold-, or yellow-striped patterns across my handsome black back. I prefer to live in the higher elevations, more like 4,000 to 8,000 feet above sea level, in the mountains among the oaks and evergreens. Like the diamondback, my bite is poisonous. After all, we're **pit vipers**. That's how the good Lord made us. So, be forewarned.

I stick to the ground and, with the exception of gobbling up certain **prey** like mice and lizards — a fellow does need to eat, doesn't he? — I avoid others. But I do get around — into caves and burrows, under bushes, crossing a dirt road or, in some cases, sunbathing on the steps of a cabin.

So, I can share with you a few short vignettes about my fellow non-human creatures for whom this forest is home. And, because some humans have a cabin here in these woods, I have chosen to share some stories about our run-ins with them.

And just as an FYI, all the words in our stories that pertain to us are in the *Glossary* and typed in **bold**. If you want to check the definitions, the **Glossary** is after our *End — and Beginning Chapter.* Some of us are typed in **bold** by name, and you can also find a brief description of us in the *Brief Description section*, which follows the *Glossary*.

The words you see typed in italics, like *crotalos cerberus* (that's me), are the Latin names for us. That is the language in which all plants and animals are put into categories. Why? I don't know. I'm just here to tell you what I've been observing in my neighborhood.

Feel free to keep a notebook close by so you can take notes or make your own drawings. And also check our website, www.NuggetPress.com.

I hope you enjoy meeting some of my people as they encounter some of your people.

Signed,

Mr. Arizona Black Rattlesnake

= SPRING =

It's been a quiet winter here in the National Forest. The black bears **hibernate**. They go into their solitary caves and sleep the whole winter long.

Don't you feel like doing that sometimes?

They don't even come out to eat or go to the bathroom. But FYI, I don't think they even go to the bathroom all winter. They just sleep.

Me? I find a warm spot underground and "slow down." We black rattlers huddle and cuddle and slither all together into a kind of keep-warm lovefest, while asleep. Some experts do call it **hibernation**. That's okay.

Some birds go south. They "winter" in such places as Guatemala. The tiny little hummingbirds fly all the way to south-central Mexico. Red-tailed hawks, on the other hand, prefer the golf courses of Scottsdale, Arizona. The robins generally hang out somewhere else in the "lower 48," often east of here. Even the experts are not entirely sure about the robins.

Some just tough it out. The Steller's jay stays here. The white-tailed deer "bed" under as much cover as they can find, hunkering close together. The **javelina** (pronounced "hava-leena") cluster together or find nooks and caves in the mountainside.

But I digress.

A Rattler's Tale

It's spring. Let's see who is about, and what kinds of encounters they might be having with that family of humans that just drove their Bronco up the rocky dirt road to their cabin for the weekend.

SCOOPING UP THE RIP-STOP

We're in the mountains, at about 6,500 feet in altitude, and my habitat is next to a seasonal creek. "Seasonal" means that sometimes the creek flows and sometimes it doesn't.

This remote spot is very close to the headwaters of the mighty "Turkey Creek," which meanders downhill into the "Big Bug Creek," and eventually finds its way into the Verde River, which flows into the Salt River, which meets up with the Gila River (which came from the San Pedro River), which then encounters the Colorado River in western Arizona. It then officially becomes the Colorado River and, finally, what's left of it trickles — if it's not all drained off for some human purpose — into the Gulf of Mexico. My corner of the creek may not seem important to you. However, it is a matter of life and death to us.

Other useful info:

The forest is an impressive mixture of tall ponderosa, walnut, spruce, and California live oak. The **evergreens** are always green, and — it being spring — the **deciduous** trees are deciding to "go green" once again.

The afternoons are warming up. I have slithered out from a crevice in the rock wall to catch some rays. I hope the humans don't see me. I generally stay a respectful distance. More on that later. Here's today's news:

Mr. and Mrs. Red-Tailed Hawk have returned after wintering in Scottsdale. They say the bunny hunting is superior on the 14th hole. This couple build a nest in the same tree each spring. They have found last year's nest and they're fixing to spruce it up. Mrs. Hawk is expecting.

A hawk's nest can measure six feet across. It's *big*. So, they swoop and snatch and gather sticks, branches, and whatnot for what I assume will soon be a bunch of eggs and little hawks-to-be.

Here come the humans. They've already started a fire in their fireplace. I can tell because smoke is curling out of the chimney and wafting into the sky. They've stepped outside to survey the scene. Mrs. Human has something in her hand. With them are two smaller humans — their children — for a total of four.

"Can we go on a hike tomorrow?" asks the boy. "We can blaze a trail across the hill to the hiking path that leads up the mountain. Then we can say 'hi' to the ranger in the lookout tower."

"What's he do up there?" asks the girl, who thinks too highly of her older brother than is good for either of them.

"He keeps a lookout for forest fires. Duh!" says her brother, a know-it-all who does not deserve her admiration.

The human mom is down with the hike. "Sure. We can use this rip-stop nylon for marking our trail. We can cut it in strips and…."

"And tie them to branches along the path," says the girl, suddenly ready to leave right now.

"Good idea," says Mom, but let's go inside and make dinner. We have to keep the fire going if we're going to cook some burgers and s'mores tonight." She drapes the repulsive orange cloth over a fence post. I watch them clomp up the steps and disappear indoors.

Mr. & Mrs. Red-Tail continue circling in the open sky. They make it look effortless, catching the wind and cruising for a few long minutes without so much as a flap of the wings. He's concentrating on dinner — maybe a mouse or squirrel.

She, however, has other things on her mind. She knows she needs a homey abode, and she knows she's going to lay some eggs any day now. The sooner they make their nest into a comfortable lodging spot, the better.

That disgusting marigold rag catches her eye. In a flash she swoops down and grabs it in her clutches. She starts to fly back to the twiggy bower, but when she tries to dislodge the rag from her claws into the nest, it won't let go of her talons. That rip-stop nylon has a mind of its own.

She shrieks for Mr. R.T. He banks a curve and zeroes in on the colorful culprit, clamping down on the rag while she flutters and flaps. She finally pulls free. He retracts his claws more easily since the cloth is now stuck among the twigs.

When Mr. R.T. finally pulls it loose, he says to Mrs. R.T., "You *really* want this old piece of junk?"

Mrs. R.T. acknowledges that the nylon is not as nifty in the nest as it looked on the fence. She drapes it on the outside edge of the nest and cruises around the meadow looking for softer stuff. Mr. R.T. sails up into the sky, still on the lookout for dinner.

I get cold and slide back into the rock wall. I call it a night.

In the morning, the four humans gather at the pole and look for the piece of ragged rip-stop. The boy asks, "Where did the rag go?" The mom looks puzzled. Then the dad looks toward the sky and sees this strip of orange flapping off the edge of the nest, about 75 feet above ground in the tall pine. He laughs and shows the boy and girl how to lean slightly backwards without falling over, so they can look too.

Mrs. Human is disgruntled, but resourceful. She goes into the cabin and returns with the remains of some old cotton shirt that will easily tear into strips. But — and here is where I confess that they're not all bad, those particular humans — she also brings out something that looks really fluffy. "I found a torn pillow," she says. "I guess the hawks will need something softer than rip-stop nylon if they're going to lay eggs and have a family." She lays it out on the ground near the fence.

That's a rather good end to this close encounter. The humans blaze their trail. Mrs. R.T. spots the stuffing and scoops it up for the nest. In a few weeks, you hear the high-pitched squawks of the new baby hawks.

STEALING THE GARBAGE

Here in the forest, we all try to get along. We practice what you might call 'animal etiquette'.

I admit, there is that business of **predator-eat-prey**. But for the most part, we give each other space and respect each other's territory. We abide by the rules that seem to have been laid out by some Great Creator Spirit who wants us all to live in balance in His forest.

The humans visit just *some* of the time. It is *not* their home. And we're talking deep in the National Forest, so there's not likely to be a plow or backhoe destroying our habitat, ripping down trees for yet another human takeover. So, these particular humans seem, on the surface of it all, not too destructive.

They have put up signs around the edge of their little slice of paradise that say, "Wilderness Stronghold." The sign, a yellow triangle, displays a spruce tree, a male deer, and a hawk. Since it is "their" property (in human terms), not too many other humans trespass.

I remind you; it is *not* their property. It is not even the property of the "National Forest Service." It is *ours*. (Well, maybe it all belongs to the Creator). But I digress.

These humans have some peculiar habits. One rather smelly habit is putting out the bag of leftovers. Leftovers? We are so much more careful not to generate waste products. Think about it: when have you seen a forest — that is, one *not* overrun by humans — cluttered with burned up tin cans, broken beer bottles, and plastic bags snagged in the locust bushes?

Never! Of course not. We clean up nice. And if the first round of **scavengers** doesn't accomplish the task, the tiny **detrivores** (aka **detritivores**) do. Termites are part of God's important plan — wood chips to wood chips.

However, the lure of human-generated garbage can cause some close encounters…

Mr. & Mrs. Human's tool shed is just a short walk from their cabin. The missus usually stores the leftovers in a bag in the shed, so it won't stink up the cabin. I get that. Very few of us make it smelly where we live. Mice are something of the exception — more on that later.

On this particular summer day, the mom had left last night's dinner and this morning's breakfast trash in the shed. Fine and good. But after breakfast she forgets to close the door to that shed. And while humans don't appear to have a keen sense of either sight (compare: hawk) or smell (contrast: bear, coyote, — and *skunk*), most of *us* do. It's how we find lunch.

A flat ledge juts out from my stone wall where a serpent can sunbathe.

10

From where I lay curled up, I can see both the back door to the cabin and the only door to the shed. On this sunny afternoon, the shed door is wide open. Since it's a warm summer day, the trash in the shed packs a pungent odor.

Suddenly, the lady skunk wanders into view, her nose in the air. Here, in the forest, we know her as "Rose." She's caught the scent, all right, and she's heading just where she really oughtn't to head — the shed.

But in the open door she goes. I listen to her rustle for grub, pawing that bag of leftovers. It has to be just about as tall as she is because I catch a glimpse of her on her hind legs, front paws over the edge of the bag. Then I see her knock it over and grab a lettuce leaf from the stuff strewn on the floor.

Unfortunately, just at that moment, Mrs. Human decides to take some scrapings from lunch out to the trash bag in the shed. She's just minding her own business — which is not a good idea in the forest, where you never know who you might encounter.

Into the shed saunters Mrs. H. with a plate of scraps. It's shady in the shed, and she has to adjust her eyesight to the darkness. It takes a second, and then I hear the "Gasp!" She has suddenly encountered Rose, who sports a bountiful mouthful of greens dangling from her jaws.

Just so you understand the dynamics, please remember that even though it is our forest, and you humans are the invaders, we know quite well that to go into a human-made structure is a fool's errand. (Most of us, anyway — see "Sneaking up on Contraband," later). It's dangerous. A no-no.

And humans seem to be acutely aware of a skunk's reputation.

Rose is quite conscious that she has committed a *big* trespass.

Mrs. Human is rightfully terrified.

Both stare at each other, frozen with fear.

Will Mrs. H. bring the plate down on the skunk's head?

Will Rose emit her special sprinkle against human aggression?

As it turns out, both have good sense. Both realize this does not have to be a lose-lose. Mrs. H. knows she has entered the shed by *surprise*. Rose knows she has *trespassed*. Mrs. H. steps back — a gesture of deference. Rose scoots out of the shed, declining to spray — a courtesy if ever there was one — and runs down the hill.

This story would have a happy enough ending if it just ends like that. But there is a short last chapter. Mrs. H. decides that just a few leftovers might be placed strategically down-hill by the creek, in case another mother seeks supper for her children.

"COME FLY WITH ME"

This is one for the birds. I mean *really*!

I could tell you a lot of tales about the many birds that frequent this forest. There are the handsome Steller's jays — one look is never enough. The feisty rufous hummingbirds dive-bomb each other even if there are two feeders to share. Talk about back-stabbers! The robins add color as they return in the spring and sip at the creek. The woodpeckers and warblers, the bank starts with their flashy red/white/black colors — they're all part of the scene. I like them all. The small ones make a good supper.

Occasionally someone shows up who's not from here. He's a wild one, but this ain't his turf. He belongs elsewhere. His main territory is a different part of the big U. S. of A.

And so it is, on this warm spring weekend, that a Great-Tailed Grackle lands on the ponderosa branch near the cabin.

You need to understand. The GTG, as I'll call him, is unfamiliar with our forest. His main territory is Texas, with periodic wanderings west into New Mexico. Rarely does he scout for a mate as far away as central Arizona. So, imagine my surprise when I see him from a distance, claws firmly grabbing a branch twenty feet from the cabin porch and whistling his heart out at what seems to be the object of his affections.

To the untrained eye, they appear to have a lot in common. He is black, with glistening feathers, about a foot tall from head to toe, plus another good foot of tail feathers below his body. Nearly two feet tall, from top to tail.

She stands about two feet tall as well — black, eyes gleaming, alert and attentive.

But this romance is not to be. For *he* is a bird — and *she* is a dog.

She's the black heeler/lab mix that the family has brought with them for the weekend. She stands firmly at the edge of the porch, barking a loud "woof, woof," like dogs do, at this bird. She calls "Stranger, danger!" over and over, and over. *Ad nauseum.*

Mr. GTG is screeching his most charming song, flapping his wings wide and spreading his tail. He is very handsome. He is displaying his best wares — and he is coming on to her!

But she will have none of it. She just barks — without ceasing. After all, *she* is a dog, and *he* is a bird!

I would write this off as a bit of unusual forest craziness but for this: Mr. GTG stays for a good ten minutes on Saturday. Ten minutes of a GTG love song — "Whistle, Rattle, Crack" versus "Woof, woof" is a long time, in bird and dog life, and to snake ears. It just goes on and on. Mr. GTG will not leave. And Ms. Doggie will not stop defending her human family's front porch. That is surely enough of an encounter, if it just stops there.

However, Mr. GTG returns and exhibits the same passionate courtship routine on Sunday morning. He seems to beg the dog, "Come Fly with Me!" He must be *really* desperate to find a mate.

But that dog, she is not the one. She continues the same "You are not my friend" argument as long as Mr. GTG persists.

Finally, after a ten-minute storm of interest — you really had to see this to believe it — Mr. GTG swoops close to the porch, flies down along the driveway, and careens off into the air. The dog, bless her heart, tears off the porch after hm, not to "come fly with me," but to chase the intruder away, in a very grounded sort of way.

I do hope Mr. GTG makes it back to Texas. He deserves better than a dog.

GALLOPING JACKALOPE

So, there I was, coiled in the grass, ready to spring on an innocent little field mouse, when a shot cracked the air, and suddenly a **Jackalope** sprang out of a nearby bush and galloped away!

Believe me? C'mon, you're not *that* gullible, I hope.

Let's get one thing straight. The Jackalope is not a real animal. I agree, he is a fun myth, and I've heard rumored around the forest that those humorous humans have even attached the horns of a deceased pronghorn antelope onto the stuffed head of a deceased hare to make it *look* like the real thing. They also send cute little "Jackalope" postcards. They even categorize him in the **taxonomy** of animals as being of the group "mythological hybrids," and of the sub-grouping called "fearsome critter." You can tell its just fake fun because it's not in Latin. Duh!

But the black-tailed jackrabbit is a real character in these woods, and we do have a tale to tell about him.

You need to understand that a jackrabbit, or a hare, is in the same **family** as a cottontail rabbit (*leporidae*), but he's a different **species** (*Lepus californicus*). He is much larger, with huge hind legs. When jumping, he looks like he's up to three feet tall. And he has enormous "rabbit" ears, almost a foot tall.

Oddly, there is a hare called the "antelope jackrabbit." Don't ask me why. He doesn't have antelope horns. He ranges around in the Sonoran Desert, not up here in the mountains, so I really don't know him personally.

Back to us. The forest has fields and meadows, as well as trees, and it's there in a bushy field where Harry the Hare hangs out. So, it happens that one day, our family of humans is hiking along a forest service road, fairly close to the field where Harry has just crouched down, munching on some twigs.

Me? I am about to attack — not a cottontail rabbit—since they don't live here. No, I've set my predatory sights on a pesky little field mouse. I am coiled, quietly — *very* quietly — ready to spring.

Suddenly, from over the hill, we hear the explosively loud "crack" of a rifle shot.

Spring is not hunting season for *anything*. And besides, this particular family and their two children do not have guns with them while walking down the dirt road.

Harry is really startled! He jumps up from his bush and bounds across the meadow into the forest.

The people, also startled, catch their glimpse of him. The boy (Mr Know-it-all) yells, "Look at that deer!"

But what deer has ears a foot high? Yes, I confess, when Harry is bounding off across the meadow with his long legs and short bobbing tail, he sort of looks like a deer. But of course, his ears are a give-away.

The sister claims one-upmanship on her brother. "No, it's not. Can't you see the ears? That's a Jackalope!"

Mom laughs. "You know Jackalopes aren't real, you guys. But you're right about the ears. We just saw a jackrabbit!"

Dad is mad. "Who in blazes is shooting off a rifle out of season? They could hurt someone."

Fortunately for all of us, we don't hear any more shots fired. Maybe that human on the other side of the mountain ridge has run out of bullets.

Unfortunately for me, I lose lunch. The field mouse startles and runs away, too. I hope I find something for dinner.

= SUMMER =

Summer in the Southwest is beautiful, but dry. Grasses sprout up in every field. Delicate white flowers bloom among the locust bush thorns. The apple trees, planted alongside the creek decades ago by the first white humans in this neighborhood, bud into thousands of apples — green, gold and red. Those early humans had varietal foresight.

However, the creek bed is dry. Typically, it won't rain during most of April, May and June. The rain usually arrives in July and August, during "**monsoon**" season.

However, some of the local berries are bursting on their bushes. While the wild blackberries wait another month or two before turning ripe, the juniper trees are sprouting berries galore. Prime time for bears.

JUNIPER BERRIES FOR JUNIOR

Bears don't bother me, and I don't bother them. They make enough of a lumbering noise as they shuffle through the underbrush that anyone with ears can hear them. Even a **boreal pit viper** like me. They prefer the *flora* side of the food chain.

On this particular mountainside, I'm looking for lunch and keeping well out of sight when I spot a young black bear snuffling around the juniper berries that grow in profusion among the logs felled years ago by a forest fire.

Things are going just fine. The bear is eating the berries. But that pesky dog shows up with the humans again. And, as dogs do, she gets a whiff of the bear. It's hard to miss.

The young bear snuffles around uphill. A tangled swath of prickly locust bushes forms a big briar patch barrier between Junior Bear and the dog. But that briar patch does not deter this self-appointed watch hound from sending out the alarm. "Woof, woof," all over again. "Stranger, danger!" in the most urgent and annoying manner.

Fortunately, Mr. Human approaches the dog, looks uphill, and spots Junior Bear. Mr. H. has the good sense to call Mrs. H., who removes Herr Watch Dog to the inside of the cabin.

Then it becomes a matter of who will blink first. Mr. H. stands transfixed, fascinated that one of the most solitary residents of our forest has chosen to show up on "his" hillside.

Junior, who doesn't have much experience in the human being department, stands by his juniper berries, also transfixed.

Junior just wants to eat the berries within reach and, at the same time, he is curious about this two-legged **predator** with eyes in the front of his head who just stands there, rudely gaping. Meanwhile, the third predator with eyes in front, the determined watch dog, has been removed (thank goodness) from the battlefield.

Bear and man conduct a serious stare-down for some time. Then Junior Bear blinks, sniffs the wind, and lumbers off. He's eaten all the berries in that patch anyway.

I hope this doesn't happen again. By the time a bear grows up to adulthood, if he is allowed that opportunity, he'll learn that most humans shoot to kill. Humans seem to think it's a big thrill to kill a bear from a distance by rifle fire. Let them try wrestling a bear, where the odds are more equal, *mano a mano*, paw to paw, and see how they like it.

TUMBLING FROM THE NEST

I don't know why it is, but among the thousands of trees in our forest, some birds unfailingly pick the front porch instead as their prime location for a nest. It could be because the wooden beam is close up under the roof and not readily seen by scavengers.

This summer a Western bluebird decides to make her nest under the eaves, on a sturdy wide beam out of the common view. It's unlikely that a hawk or jay can steal her eggs.

For Mrs. B.B., who is mostly a soft buff gray compared to her handsome bluer mate, this looks like an ideal location. She makes a nest with twigs and grasses and a few stray threads from that carrot-colored rip-stop nylon Mrs. Human left on the fence post nearby.

It has been a busy day. Three of the four eggs cracked open yesterday. Mr. and Mrs. B.B. are busily bringing bugs and worms to eager beaks. To-day, three little fledglings have begun the bold adventure of learning to fly. They've all made it and have set off flying — low to the ground at first, then landing on bushes and fence posts near the nest. Mama Blue watches them with pride.

But there is still the fourth, who pecks his egg open later than the others and who seems to be struggling with the perennial dilemma, "To fly or not to fly, that is the question."

Since this patch of ground is part of my regular beat, I'm curled up discreetly among the edgy rocks that constitute a nearby wall. I'm warming myself in the afternoon heat, but also thinking about what might occur if that baby bird falls out of the nest. You know that old Black Rattlesnake saying, "A bird on the ground is worth two in the nest."

Things might go along smoothly, with Mama Blue hovering nearby and encouraging number four, while he awkwardly flutters and flounces his way toward airborne flight.

Instead, up walks Mrs. Human. She has seen the nest before, and today she hears the tiny "eep, eep" coming from Junior Blue.

"Hey, little bird," she says, as she climbs onto a plastic chair to be eye level with the nest. She cups her hand under the little guy as if to pick him up and help him get going.

In a panic, he flops away from her hand and falls to the ground in front of the cabin porch. After a few seconds of lying in the dirt, completely still, he begins a tender little flutter of his wings. It appears that he was stunned more than hurt. For a small bird like that to fall eight feet to the ground, when he is still just a ball of fluff and almost lighter than air, is actually not as bad as it appears.

The human mom jumps off the chair in surprise, one foot catching the edge of a hoe, which swings up and bonks her in the back of the head. She looks at the horror of what she has done. This poor baby bird, who had been cautiously testing its abilities in the nest, is now exposed to the elements — such as me — and remains unable to fly.

"I'm so sorry, little bird," Mrs. H. murmurs in dismay. She feels guilty. She should. She doesn't help this little chick; she endangers it.

From the rock wall, I consider a sly move. Baby Blue would make a great snack.

Suddenly, Mama Blue dive-bombs me and swoops toward the ground with a great hue and cry, "pew, pew," followed by a hard bluebird-style chattering. She mews and chatters constantly, fluttering to the ground, then returning to a nearby branch. She is not going to let this little guy become snake bait. He needs to learn to fly — *fast* — or he'll be my dinner.

Baby Blue flounces and flops. Once, twice. He bumbles down the road a few inches. Mama Blue clucks at him in her most urgent mother-knows-best voice. Mrs. H. stands on the porch, not saying anything and thank goodness, not doing anything *else* stupid.

I watch this drama unfold with mixed feelings. As I mentioned, he could provide me with just the snack to make it through the night. On the other hand, I love to see little critters overcome obstacles — especially when faced with the challenge of human interference.

Baby Blue flops his body and flaps his wings, barely lifting himself off the ground. He rolls a few more inches further down the pathway. Mama Blue goes "mew, mew" and flaps her wings. She does not dive down to him, but she *does* stay nearby.

This routine repeats itself five or six times. The fledgling tries his darnedest, and Mama Blue chatters encouragement. With each effort his fluffy little wings seem to lift his fluffy little body further off the ground — an inch, three inches, each time he remains "airborne" — until he lands on the road again, another foot or two away from where he started. For all I know (I don't speak Bluebird) Mama Blue might be giving him pointers.

Finally, after many minutes and many flops, Junior Blue gives a mighty heave of his tiny wings and manages to lift himself aloft. He flies to a nearby railing on the fence. Mama Blue joins him. Then, after a short rest, she flies to a nearby branch. Little Blue follows her. He is flying on his own!

I'm sure you get my point about Mrs. Human. Just because you're a mom in one **species** does *not* mean you know anything about being a mom in another species. When it comes to teaching a baby bird to fly, unless she is properly taught, Mrs. Human should leave it to Mrs. Western Bluebird.

LOST AND SCARED

I don't have to contend with many natural **predators**. Generally, I'm rather good at defending myself, staying out of harm's way, and acting as the predator instead of the **prey**. The only creatures in this forest I fear are the deer, **javelina**, and mountain lion. The mountain lion would pounce and eat me in a heartbeat.

The problem with deer and javelina is that when they stomp on a snake, it's curtains for the snake. They don't want to eat me (they are both mostly **herbivores**), but they would kill me if they found me in their way. If I were to bite them, it would be curtains for them!

Enter — a horse — and his hooves.

Horses? They are domesticated! They live where people live. Why worry about them here in the National Forest? I should be able to live my life without worrying about horses stomping on me.

So, you can imagine my fear when that human family comes to the 'hood one day leading a *horse* with a halter and a lead rope. Huh? This is the woods, not the paddock! I slither back into the bushes to stay beyond reach.

Turns out, the mom and dad have planned to bring two horses to the cabin in our woods for a week. They've rented a trailer and hooked it to the back of their Bronco. They have packed extra hay, halters, bridles, hobbles and tethers in the special trailer.

On their way in from the highway — truth *can* be stranger than fiction — an **American Quarter horse** steps out of the underbrush onto the United States Forest Service road, begging to be found.

How come?

Every Fourth of July weekend there is a pow-wow and rodeo in the nearby city. People bring their horses from all around the region to compete in calf-roping, barrel-racing, cutting and penning, and even dressage.

Some of the pow-wow participants camped in the forest that past weekend and tied their horses on hobbles to munch the forest grass. All that was normal.

What was *not* normal was that on the night after the rodeo, a huge thunderstorm broke open the sky. All of us natives knew how to find our caves and burrows and duck for cover. But there was one horse — a city horse — who broke loose from his hobble in a panic and bolted further into the woods. The next day his humans looked but couldn't find him. They gave up — rather callously, I would say — and returned to the city. The horse (a city horse, I remind you) was left alone — alone, lost and afraid.

So, on this weekend in the middle of July, following the pow-wow, Mr. and Mrs. Human find the horse. He is *soooo* glad to be found! That's a sure sign that he is not *wild*, like us. We *do not* want to be found by humans.

He stands and waits while Mr. H takes a harness and lead, slips them over his head, and then walks him to the cabin. Dad runs a few lines of cable between some trees, clips a carabiner to one of the lines, and hooks up a tether to the horse so he can feed, but not break free and get lost again.

Honestly, this city horse looks gaunt and tired. He's been lost for over a week. It's a good thing they found him. If they hadn't, he probably would have starved or been attacked by the local mountain lion. Domestic critters really can't survive here in the wild without that irritating human presence. And by the way, what a great meal that would have made for the lion, the coyote, the hawks, and other carnivores. Maybe there even would have been a bite or two for me.

I hear them call him "Blaze." He's a dark sorrel with white lightning marking his forehead. They feed him hay and alfalfa pellets. He even lies down, something uncommon to horses (they can sleep standing up). Me — I'd rather curl up in a dark nook or burrow.

At first, I worry about him stomping on me. I stay clear, but I realize that he is really worn out from trying to survive in the wild. He's too tired to be startled when I glide up closer for a good look. So, this particular encounter causes no harm to me, and it saves the life of that horse.

The family keeps him at their cabin for a week. They even bring in two other horses from a ranch. Everyone has a chance to ride each horse, but "Blaze" is the hands-down favorite. The boy and girl brush him and feed him like he's really special.

I don't get it — after all, if they hadn't rescued this city-slicker, he probably would have died. I could handle a week alone without human intervention just fine — I'd prefer it.

And besides, "Blaze" could end my life in a flash. One misstep and I'm toast! That whole week I avoid the meadow where he stands peacefully nibbling grass in the sun.

SNEAKING UP ON CONTRABAND

Don't blame me. They've probably taught you the old story in the Bible about how my ancestors tempted Eve to eat from the tree of knowledge. Sounds like the right thing to do if you're going to get by in the world.

But I'm not a fan of skittering willy-nilly toward something just because it's tempting, *especially* if you don't know what it is.

In the summertime I do hustle around at night when it's still warm. I have encountered all of our **crepuscular** and **nocturnal** friends. Each one is unique.

For instance, Rocky Raccoon. He's pretty much a nighttime kind of guy, solitary, **omnivorous** (plants and whatever **vertebrates** he might ingest), with excellent night vision, and a great sense of smell.

That is what gets Rocky into trouble. I've been around a few seasons, so I know that, among other things, whatever the humans leave on their porch is really off-limits. Out-of-bounds. *Verboten*, Ix-nay. A no-no.

On this particular summer night Mr. Human and a pal stand on the porch taking in the full moon, having a smoke. Why they think this is a good habit I'll never know. But they each smoke a cigarette or two, engaging in a lengthy philosophical conversation about nature and the wilderness (like they know what they're talking about), and man's place in the universe. Seems they think the universe revolves around human beings. Such a sad self-deception. In any case, they finally grow tired of their brilliant ramblings and call it a night.

Most humans never see us. These hillsides sport an abundance of camouflage — trees, bushes, flowers, and grasses — so we can hide from you. The **diurnal** humans miss almost everything that goes on at night. Enter our **nocturnal** friend Rocky Raccoon.

Some of us do get tempted. And so, it is on this balmy summer night, after the last dusty pinks have faded in the western sky and the myriad of stars has begun to twinkle despite the brightness of the moon, that young Rocky decides to see for himself if that powerful scent represents a possible treasure over there on the human porch.

Rocky has several positive attributes. In addition to that cute-looking mask across his face, he has incredibly dexterous front paws, almost like a human's. I'd say better than a bear's. Way superior to the coyote, deer, or jack rabbit. He can grab something and fiddle with it, maybe even open a closed box and dig out what's inside. He also has a very keen sense of smell.

But this sense of smell can get Rocky into trouble, too. He seems to have caught the odor of tobacco and is determined to go after it.

Since I am potential prey for Rocky, I don't go out of my way to warn him. I watch from under a thorn bush as he prances up the cabin steps. The cigarettes smell stronger! Being the self-designated smart guy that he thinks he is, he soon realizes that the bright colored packet on the table is the potential pot of gold. He hops up onto a chair, then onto the table, and grabs that pack of Marlboros in his dexterous little front paws. He rips open the package and grabs a few of those white-wrapped cylinders of tobacco. Then, overcome by temptation, he stuffs them into his little raccoon mouth with his sharp little raccoon teeth. He bites into them and starts to chew.

43

Arrggghhh! I can tell he has abruptly learned the deep dark truth about tobacco — it tastes awful! What is he to do? He's desperate to spit out the gunk, but he has also sunk his claws into that treasure trove. He hops off the table, pack of cigarettes speared to one paw, and scurries toward the creek. He shakes the pack off the claws of his front foot, and dips both paws in the water. He drinks, spits, and barfs. Then a few more gulps of clear water, and this young wizard hurries back to his den upstream.

By the way, the people come out the next morning and can't find their smokes. Only later does the dad wander down to the creek and find a totally trashed pack of soggy cigs. I don't expect he'll be leaving them out on the porch after that close encounter.

= AUTUMN =

The first thing to know about early autumn in Arizona is that we're still in the **monsoon** season. It rains almost every afternoon as the clouds collide into the mountains. In a matter of mere minutes, the creek changes from bone dry to a gentle trickle. Suddenly, a swooshing wall of water sweeps by, almost two feet tall — a real flash flood! Then it calms down and becomes a normal creek.

Second, nights turn crisp. I really must catch the sun when I can and then burrow into a hole or cave or match up with other rattlers to share body heat.

With those frosty nights, the leaves begin to turn — first the aspens with their gold and the auburn oaks. It's startlingly bright, especially against the cerulean blue sky.

Most birds are 'on the wing.' The robins fly somewhere. Mr. and Mrs. Red-Tail Hawk head for Scottsdale.

The days and nights are pointing toward a chilly winter when a heavy snowfall prevents the humans from driving down that Forest Service road to their cozy cabin. But, until then….

STRIKE? OR SLITHER?

I suppose it's time I tell you of *my* close encounter with — *your* kind.

Just because some old man told it one way in the Bible, it isn't necessarily so. The Indigenous Peoples' stories give us serpents more respect and appreciation. After all, we are all part of the Great Spirit's magnificent creation.

First things first. Who lives in these hills and valleys year-round? From the desert to the mountains, this land is my land. It belongs to me and a lot of other animals. Humans are definitely the invasive species.

We could co-exist peacefully if you tried harder. I mean, we rattlesnakes come out on the land primarily to find food. And as cold-blooded **ectotherms**, we **reptiles** do need to "take the sun" on a regular basis. But we do not try to bother human beings.

My kin have lived in this forest for thousands of years. I have brothers and sisters, cousins, children and grandchildren, nieces and nephews in the surrounding miles up and down the nearby creek.

Over the years, humans have not treated us kindly. My uncle suffered a dire fate one day when the boys and men were returning from a "hunting" trip and found him curled up, minding his own business, under a ramp that leaned against a stone wall.

Did it matter that Mrs. H. had been traipsing up and down the ramp all morning while they were out brandishing rifles? Did it matter that, while she was carrying firewood down that ramp to a log pile near the house, my uncle dozed the entire time, leaving her completely and safely alone?

No! When they came back from their hunt — empty handed, I might add — they found my uncle and blew his head off.

And then there was the time that my cousin was sunbathing on the steps to their porch. They took his life with an axe. They tacked his body to the roof, and he twitched for hours while the blood drained out of his body. It was ghastly. They say snakes don't actually feel pain — that the post-mortem twitching is just a nervous reaction. It wasn't my death, so I can't tell you, but just hearing about it made me feel his pain.

You humans should have known that a rag saturated with ammonia would have done the trick. If you put out the ammonia, we leave. Simple as that. But no, the macho men had to strut their stuff.

Maybe we need to start a movement — Black Rattlesnakes Matter! Diamondbacks do too, but at least they have a baseball team named after them. I'm not asking much. Just a little respect.

Word gets around in the forest. You humans may not hear it, much less understand it, but the trees, the crows, the squirrels and coyotes — they all talk. They spread the word. The word is not comforting.

So, I suffer a huge sense of alarm one summer afternoon when, as I am about to cross the dirt road, Mrs. Human shows up, walking with her dog. If I could bark, I would. I would yell, "Stranger, danger!"

The dog behaves better than usual that day. She stops and barks only twice. She does not come over to check me out. I think she suspects that something out of the ordinary is up. Yes — it's my tail, rattling a warning like crazy!

Despite my irritation at being interrupted, I do what I was bred to do. I warn Mrs. H. and Ms. Doggie. I raise my head to keep a beady eye on her and I raise my tail and I rattle. I rattle again. (FYI, my rattle moves at about 60 RPS — rattles per second). I'm displaying my potential, but at the same time showing respect. Just a "heads up," as it were. You leave me alone; I'll leave you alone. Pretty decent behavior, given that she is the intruder.

Immediately the dog barks again. Thank goodness she doesn't run at me because I'd have had to take her out. Dogs are, after all, a natural **predator**. Sometimes they're dumb, but they're also dangerous.

Mrs. H. hears my rattle, looks up and notices me. I am curled in the grass by the edge of the road, head and tail aloft and alert. Great, I've warned her. I am *here*. I was here *first*. Do *not* come any closer!

Mrs. H. stops her walk. She starts talking to me in a calm, measured voice. No hysteria — no need. She is, after all, way beyond my striking distance.

"Hi, Mr. Rattlesnake," she says (I'm making this up — I don't understand human — but the tone sounds a lot like she *might* be saying something like this).

"Mr. Rattler, I'm holding my dog right here. We're going to stay put. Why don't you just keep on crossing the road? Then you can slide back into the grass and bushes where we are *not* planning to walk, and you can go on home. No harm, no foul, okay?"

Well, for all the world, it does seem like she's granting me the respect I deserve. She stays rooted on her spot, still as can be, with the dog's collar in her hand. Still, I didn't quite trust her. After all, she's human.

I decide to cross the road. I do it with dignity. I slither, kind of like a side-winder (distant relative), but I keep my head high and my eyes on her at all times. My thin yellow-white strips glisten brightly across my beautiful black scaly back. Respect, but not exactly trust. Slither, sidewind, stare. Slither, sidewind, stare.

She doesn't move. Finally, I make it to the other side of the road, which is my direction home, and I disappear into the grass. No harm, no foul. A win-win.

From either side you can call *that* a close encounter with respect.

THOSE PESKY RODENTS

The **voles** (aka field mice) and I have an ambivalent relationship. I admire their ability to scarf food out of a cardboard canister and slip cheese out of a mousetrap without a scratch. They can jump, run and even swim. I can't. But I am **predator**, and they are **prey**. As far as I'm concerned, their highest purpose in life is to serve as dinner for me.

Like me, they also have an ambivalent relationship with the humans. The children think they are just adorable. The adults, on the other hand, don't. The parents have seen the mice steal the mattress stuffing, shed droppings in teacups, and generally leave messy mousy swaths of destruction. Furthermore, mice are **nocturnal**, which means they scurry about nibbling graham crackers after the Coleman lanterns have been turned off for the night.

"Aww, it's so cute," I hear one of the children say to the mom one day. (I happen to be hiding out in a nearby woodpile, spying on a stray lizard.) "Can't we keep it in the house and play with it? We could keep it in a cage. *Puleeze*? Can we?"

Well, the short answer is "no," but the mom tries to explain why.

"You've seen the damage they do," she says. "They leave their poop everywhere. They ate part of *every graham cracker* we left out last night."

"But Mom, isn't it funny how they **scavenged** some of our Lego blocks and put them in their nest?"

"No," she counters. "Look at the mattress stuffing and — oh my gosh, what's this?" She picks up the mop. Where there should have been long gray strands of string to clean the human floor, little nubs of dirty cotton cling to the metal clamp. "They stole the whole mop!"

It's amusing how humans don't really like mice. The two **species** are a lot alike. They both scoot around like busybodies. They both make a fuss about having a good bed to sleep in — people at night, mice during the day. They both gossip. You can hear the humans talk, talk, talk. And you can hear the mice "squeak, squeak, squeak."

They both act for selfish interests without regard to others. Mice will ruin anything human if, in their search, they can find food or bedding. Humans test drugs on mice in labs, — they don't mind destroying the little rodents for their own benefit.

Despite our differences, mice and I have a lot in common. They figure out how to use and make what they need. They burrow into holes in the ground. I don't mind burrowing into a mouse burrow for a nap.

But, very much unlike me, mice seem obsessed with entering the human cabin. What's with that? Do field mice really want to be cabin mice? No, I think it's a more basic instinct. They're trying to avoid *me*. Plus, they want warmth and comfort, just like humans. They'll curl up in a kitchen drawer for the whole winter. But OMG do they leave a stink behind (in contrast to almost all the rest of us — remember "*STEALING THE GARBAGE*"?).

Unlike their **predator** enemy, the bald eagle, field mice are not an endangered species. Thank goodness for that. I'm all for mouse overpopulation, because it's much easier for both the eagle and me to catch dinner. I might even help those humans rid their cabin of those pesky rodents.

ATTACK ON THE APPLES

I try to look on the bright side. So, despite your species' negative attributes, I appreciate the fact that about fifty years ago your human predecessors planted apple trees along the creek. It is a domesticated but delightful improvement on this wild patch of paradise.

In fall the apples come ripe — first the Golden Delicious, then the Galas, then the Granny Smiths. If the humans are visiting, they harvest the apples.

I'm basically a **carnivore**, so the apples, as a food, don't interest me. But I appreciate the elaborate food chain that keeps all sorts of us wild animals alive so that some of them *are* food for me. Insects eat fallen apples. A careless bird swoops down on the insects. I'm curled in a local tree stump, waiting for the bird, and — whammo!

Javelina love apples. I don't know if the plural of "javelina" is "javelina," "javelinae," or "javelinas." I just know they aren't pigs. I thought you should know, too.

Javelina love the mountains. They need a water source, so they stay close to the creek. They travel in packs down the dry wash where branches of nearby bushes and low-lying trees create camouflage.

On this particular fall afternoon, a pack of javelina(s?) has a group face-off with Mr. and Mrs. You-Know-Who and their children.

The whole human family has taken a hike during the early afternoon. When they return, they decide it's a good time to pick apples.

With your arms and hands, you humans have an unfair advantage — you can pluck ripe but ready apples off the tree. Today, the whole family is in on it — the dad, the mom, the boy and the girl. They've even let their pesky dog trot along. And, as usual, they are clueless about who else is around and about. For example, they do not know that I am nestled in the love grass, just soaking up a few rays before calling it a day.

They also do not know that about twenty javelina (javelinae?) are trotting down the creek bed toward the apple trees!

Suddenly, the dog does her dog thing: "Stranger danger!" ("Woof, woof!")

Trust me, a fight with a javelina is ugly. Two of their main **predators** are mountain lions and dogs. Yes, domestic dogs. They fight tusk and toe.

Suddenly, as the dog heralds the arrival of javelina, Mr. H. finally wakes up from his nature-loving reverie. What to do?

It's almost dusk and getting chilly. I'm ready to call it a day, but the opportunity to watch a dramafest keeps me glued to the grass.

Startled, Mr. H. calls, "Watch out, guys, javelina!"

Mrs. H. swings a protective arm around each child — like that will do any good. "What do we do?" she falters.

Fortunately, Mr. H. must have read up on **peccaries**. "I tell you what," he says in his 'casual' voice. "Why don't we just turn s-l-o-w-l-y around? We'll head down the meadow. We'll cross the creek and return to the cabin. Hey! We can even make fresh applesauce!"

So, the people s-l-o-w-l-y retreat. Yay. And the pack of peccaries descend upon the apple orchard for a feasting frenzy. Another close encounter that does not wind up in chaos. As Mrs. H. said to me last month, "No harm, no foul."

HIDING IN PLAIN VIEW

I'd hate to be a white-tailed deer in this national forest. Why? Because you humans have so many hunting rights to shoot them. There is the "youth-only muzzle loader" season, the regular "adult muzzle loader" season, the "CHAMP (challenged hunter access mobility permit)" season, a few brief weeks for the "archery" season, and finally, the "general" season. All in all, humans can take aim and fire from August through the end of December. What's a deer to do?

I've hissed this before. It is totally an unfair fight when the humans use guns. I suppose if a human really needs to eat, he can occasionally take down what he needs. I get that. The bow-and-arrow method seems like enough to get the job done. But with rifles from such a distance? And trophy-hunting? It removes the possibility of either "fight" *or* "flight."

Anyway, I digress.

The white-tailed deer are year-round neighbors and **herbivores**. They usually breed in January and drop their fawns around August, during or after the summer rains. The little ones stay with their moms. They usually traverse their neighborhood (several square miles), by using regular, travel-worn, near-horizontal deer paths.

Autumn is a rough time for deer. There are so many humans out here trying to bag game that their deer lives are in serious peril.

They retreat as far into the forest as possible to escape man and gun. When I slither out and about, I rarely spot a deer in this neighborhood.

Thus, one day in late autumn, I am as surprised as the humans, when they drive up their dirt driveway, to see a full family of deer standing in the parking lot, right in front of the cabin! The buck carries a full rack (of antlers, of course). Two females paw the dirt nearby. Two fawns hover tentatively close to their moms, not yet into their "teenage" rebellious stage.

This deer family mills around in the human driveway, only yards away from the steps to the cabin porch and near some edible locust bush leaves.

Why, you might ask, would there be deer in the driveway? At first, I wondered, too.

Then I figured it out. Deer want to avoid danger and be safe. They know how to move through the underbrush and use the cover of leaves, bushes, branches and other camouflage so they escape observation — and **predators**.

During hunting season, when humans move as far into the woods as possible to shoot their prey, deer strive to be where hunters are not. And one place that hunters do *not* hunt is in the open parking lot of their fellow human beings — especially the driveway of that property with the "Wildlife Refuge" sign.

So, for the deer, the driveway seems to be the perfect parking spot.

At the same time, deer are justifiably wary of humans.

So, they hold their ground uneasily as Mr. and Mrs. H. and their children drive up. The Bronco screeches to a startled halt. The humans gawk. I keep a lookout from my rock wall.

Finally, the deer acknowledge that the parking space is too small for all of them. Mr. White-Tail quickly leads his family up the hill and into a thicket. I am amazed at how fast they disappear from view.

The humans unload the car and carry supplies inside, chattering about the deer. They don't seem to grasp how being "in civilization" might, after all, be a very safe spot for a wild one's encounter — with *them*.

The deer were right about one thing: in *that* driveway, no shots were fired.

= WINTER =

Winter is quiet around here. The deer huddle close together, using body warmth against the cold. The bears **hibernate** completely for months. I retreat with my family and friends into a small cave or burrow — all of us intertwined together. Quite a snake-snuggle.

You may catch a glimpse of the coyotes out and about. They run in loose packs to take down an old deer or lost squirrel.

After a heavy snow, the forest is still. It is *our* time — the peaceful time before humans re-visit. Which reminds me, I have just two more vignettes to share in the spring that's just around the corner.

SAVED BY A BRONCO

This all happens so fast that I wouldn't believe it if you had told me. But I see it for myself.

I'm off to the side of the dirt road, catching the first sunny day of spring. I see this crazy encounter with my own elliptical beady snake-eyes. It's my story, and I'm sticking to it.

A lone deer is busily nibbling a bush that must have been overlooked last fall. She's on the downhill side of the road. A few berries hang low. Green shoots pop up from the ground looking tender and tasty.

Deer don't migrate to warmer climates during the winter. They don't **hibernate** either. They bed down together, soaking up warmth from pine needles and oak leaves. They sleep for only minute at a time. Their ears are always on high alert. They are constantly on guard. That's the sad lot in life of animals who are **prey**, and rightfully so. Just think of the critters that could feed off one downed deer. The mountain lion, bobcat, coyote, eagles, hawks, and more.

Normally deer are watchful and wary. But on this particular day in April, Mrs. White Tail must be so grateful to find a leftover batch of greens and berries that she concentrates on only one thing — food.

Meanwhile, another non-migrating, non-hibernating member of our community is out and about — the mountain lion. His *modus operandi* (way of operating) is to adapt to the harsh environment, subsisting on **voles** and rats if he must, but always on the prowl for the big one that will compensate for the harsh winter's lean food supply.

Usually he's a **crepuscular** (twilight) and **nocturnal** cat, but here he stands in broad daylight, alert and opportunistic as only a cat can be.

Mr. Mountain Lion crouches on a huge boulder uphill, up-wind, across the road from Mrs. Deer. She — uncharacteristically — does not have a clue what is about to befall her.

Mr. M. L., tail switching silently in the ready, is about to pounce.

Suddenly, from out of nowhere, that gaggle of humans careens around a rocky corner in their Bronco, driving too fast.

Startled, Mr. M. L. leaps. Equally startled, Mrs. D. freezes, exhibiting a bad case of DIHS (Deer In the Headlights Syndrome). At that moment, the Bronco screeches to a halt as Mr. M. L. lands on the hood and bounces against the windshield.

Quicker than the humans can see what almost hit them, Mr. M. L. regains his footing while still on the hood — the way that only cats can do. Then, with his big filthy front paws extended, he leaps onto the road and dashes back up the hill from whence he came. Simultaneously, Mrs. Deer awakes from her DIHS, jumps over a log and hops down the other side of the hill, disappearing deep into the underbrush.

Time stops. By sheer luck, Mr. M. L.'s fall has not broken the windshield. But his 100+ pound body has made a serious dent in the hood. From where I lay, I think I can hear human hearts thumping and lungs pumping. Slowly, they recover from the surprise and Mr. H. drives toward the cabin.

Like I say, I wouldn't believe it if I hadn't seen it with my own eyes.

THE STATE MAMMAL ESCAPES

A few minutes later, embarrassed by their brush with the woods' most agile **predator**, the startled four pull up to the steps of their cabin. I have slid quickly over to a ledge outside the east windows. I'm out of their sight, but they are in mine. Mrs. H. grabs the keys and dashes up the porch steps two-at-a-time, unlocks the door, and makes a beeline to the bathroom. She needs to go!

Mr. H. hauls in firewood from the ever-plentiful fallen-log and broken-branch forest floor. He stuffs crumpled newspaper under the first clutch of kindling.

The insides of this cabin are open for any peeping snake to see. There are windows on all sides. I've seen a couch, chairs, a cabinet (the one that mice sneak into), and the magnificent fireplace built from local stone.

At the moment, however, I am on the ledge near the trail to the uphill water tank from which a length of PVC pipe lets water flow downhill to the indoor bathroom sink and flush toilet. Humans seem to like that sort of thing.

Mr. H. and the kids start a fire in the fireplace. The cabin is chilly, even at noon. They'll keep that fire burning until they blow out all the candles and turn in after dinner.

But Mrs. H. needs to use the bathroom. As you might expect, the pesky dog follows her right in. Today the dog starts its world-renowned cry of "woof, woof, *wooooof*! Stranger-Danger!" Quite irritating! But to be honest with you, it's always an accurate signal that something's afoot.

From where I lay curled in the sun, everything looks calm. But the precious doggie is causing a ruckus like you wouldn't believe. Mrs. H. just *has* to take care of business, and the dog keeps barking, even adding a rumbling growl to its repertoire.

"Hold on a minute," grumbles the mom, trying to cajole the dog into silence. It doesn't work. The dog shoves its nose right up against the vanity under the bathroom sink like a mountain lion might spring from inside.

Of course, it isn't a mountain lion. Been there, done that (see above). And besides, a mountain lion does not fit inside a bathroom vanity cabinet.

Let me elaborate.

Every state in our U. S. of A. has a state flag. And probably a state emblem. Some states even have a state flower, a state bird, and a state mammal. Probably a state fish and a state scorpion, for all I know.

Arizona does have a state reptile, a **taxonomy class** which includes snakes, lizards, crocodiles, turtles and tortoises. The powers that be in our glorious state chose a snake to be the "state reptile."

They did not, however, choose me. They chose the ridge-nosed rattle-snake, who has a limited habitat around Ft. Huachuca in southern Arizona.

Why him? He's a pathetic representative of our species, only two feet long, sort of greenish, with a gash alongside his cheek that makes him look like he was in a gang fight. They should have chosen me, the most handsome, shiny black snake in the state, almost four feet long full-grown, with stunning white, yellow or gold stripes across my back.

Or, they could have chosen the desert-oriented diamondback rattlesnake. I think he's rather pale to win the title of "state rattlesnake," but least he has a baseball team named after him. And he has the reputation of inflicting the most **envenomations** (poisonous bites) of any of the Arizona snakes. But no, they chose the "ridge-nosed." Such a shame.

Back to the bathroom.

Enter the state *mammal*. Mrs. H. finishes her business in the bathroom and hoists up her jeans. She finally turns her attention to the vanity cabinet — the focus of canine consternation. The dog is still kvetching at the cabinet's little doorknobs. So, the mom shoos the dog out of the bathroom, closes that door, and opens the vanity cabinet door.

Curled up among the Ajax and the toilet paper, like she lives in a palace, is Ramona Ringtail! The ringtail is generally a solitary and **nocturnal** mammal, and I bet she was trying to slip in a daytime nap. I'm extremely glad she is in the human house instead of out and about because, as an **omnivore**, she might have been planning to make a snack out of *me*.

If I judge simply by inter-species-tolerant criteria (as opposed to loving only my own kind), I'd say Ramona is *really* gorgeous. Short and small, only a foot or so long, generally covered with brown fur, she has cute little semi-**retractable** claws and alluring big black eyes surrounded by white circles of fur.

Her most impressive feature is a tail that is bigger, fluffier and more distinguished than her entire body — a long "poofed" item comprised of more than a dozen black and white furry rings. Hence the name "ring-tail." Something that's gotta make Mr. Ringtail swoon.

I must give Mrs. Human some credit. Now fully dressed again, she regains her composure and speaks to Ramona. Of course, she is not on a first-name basis like I am.

"Why Mrs. Ringtail," I believe I hear her say, "I am so sorry to disturb you. But now we are in the cabin and it's a good time for you to leave. Here's what I'm going to do. I will reclose this vanity door for just a moment," (and she leans down and does so). "Then I'll open the window above the sink," (and she leans over the sink and does that). "Finally, I am going to — quickly — open your door and leave. Don't follow me. I'll close the bathroom door. When I do that, you can hop up on the sink and scoot out the window. Okay?"

Of course, it's okay. In rapid succession, Mrs. H. opens the vanity door, walks over to the bathroom door, opens it, steps outside into the living room, and closes it against an imaginary ringtail attack.

From my vantage point, Ramona Ringtail seems a bit kerflummoxed. All she had wanted was a good day's nap. It has been seriously cut short by the arrival of the humans. She is not buddies with them. But there's Mrs. Human. She has come — and she has gone. She has not exhibited any sort of **predatory** behavior and she has left Ramona an avenue of escape.

The official state mammal of Arizona leaps with agility to the sink, then to the window-sill. She glances with nostalgia around the room. I think she knows it will be the last time she ever tries to commandeer *this* castle for a state mammal snooze. Then, with a flick of her (I must say, *magnificent*) tail, she slips outside the open window, hops onto the ground, and runs like a ringtail into the forest. She is so preoccupied with her escape that she does not notice me. Yay.

Mrs. H. probably keeps her promise and returns a while later to close the vanity door, air out the room, and close the window. I don't honestly know. After those two close encounters, all in one day, I've had enough excitement. I slither back through the grass to the rock wall.

THE END....AND THE BEGINNING

So, there you have it, a cluster of vignettes in which I witness some close encounters between us and you, and one of your doggies and one of your horses. I hope you noticed that under no circumstance did any of us go beyond what the Great Creator has set us upon this earth to do — except for that dumb raccoon, Rocky, but I think he has learned his lesson. And, for the most part, these particular humans are pretty decent visitors to our neighborhood.

I hope you will glean, from this small sampling, that you humans can do the right thing. If you *must* act as a **predator**, take only what you need. Don't be arrogant or greedy. Be considerate of other species and our forest. If you can follow that golden rule, then you're welcome to come visit. But remember, it's *our* home.

AUTHOR'S NOTE

After having encountered so many of our forest friends in the wild — in their natural habitat — I wanted not only to describe some amusing or poignant stories, but also to show a realistic drawing of each animal. I was fortunate to meet Lauren Sarantopulos, an artist with the gifts of both artistic ability and sensitivity to the nature of the creatures she has portrayed. These illustrations provide both a visual tidbit of the story and a representation of the true nature of each one of God's wonderful creatures.

All of these stories have an element of truth. The setting is real, the appearance of the humans is real. The presence of all these animals is real. Some of the details are somewhat embellished.

I have learned about one change. The habitat of the great-tailed grackle has expanded since the time that Mr. GTG tried to woo Ms. Doggie by the cabin. Then, his territory was primarily Texas and some of New Mexico. These days, the habitat of the great-tailed grackle has spread throughout almost all the entire southwest. Maybe Mr. GTG would have better luck this time around.

Nancy Hicks Marshall

CRITTER QUESTIONS

1. Which animal in *A Rattler's Tale* do you like the best? Why? Do you identify with them in some way? How?

2. *A Rattler's Tale* is supposed to be about encounters between wild animals and people, but two stories are about a horse and a dog. Should these be included? Why or why not?

3. If you were writing a similar story, how would you do it? Just one animal and a continuous story about that animal? Or the story from the point of view of one of the humans? Or from the point of view from another animal — wild or domestic?

4. Which of the vignettes seemed most likely to be true? Not true? Why?

5. What two categories in the Taxonomy Chart (page 93) do all our critters (even the humans) have in common? What do these categories mean in English?

6. Three of the animals on the website (www.NuggetPress.com) have "*dactyla*" at the end of their class identifying name. Which are they, and what do they have in common?

7. What is the major difference between the Arizona Black Rattlesnake and all the other animals?

8. Which two animals use a scent or odor from their own body? Do they use it for the same purpose?

9. There are three birds in *A Rattler's Tale*. Which one soars?

10. Which animals in *A Rattler's Tale* are predators? Which are prey? Are there any animals that are neither?

For more questions and the answers to these, go to **www.NuggetPress.com** and click on the ACTIVITY section.

EXPLORE MORE – LEARN MORE

Here are some suggested projects to continue the wild animal adventure. Some Resources on the following pages might help.

1. Writing: Pick an animal you know whether wild or domestic. Write a short story from this animal's point of view. Describe them, their habitat, what food they like, whether they are predator or prey, and what's going on in their daily life. If you feel inspired, write a chapter book with at least three chapters.

2. Do a research project on the original *Cerberus*. What kind of animal was he? (Hint — he was not a rattlesnake). What was the story of Cerberus and when was it written?

3. Learn about all the snakes in your state. Compare and contrast them as to length and different features (stripes, diamonds, etc.) on their bodies, whether they are poisonous, kinds of habitat, what they eat, whether any of them is an endangered species, and what can be done to restore their population.

4. Rhymes: Write a short poem for some of the animals, making sure you find a word to rhyme with their name.

5. Study the difference between a raptor and other winged birds, such as the difference between the red-tailed hawk and the grackle or bluebird.

6.   Learn about which animals in your state are subjected to hunting seasons (hint: usually some ducks, other birds, fish, deer, or other large animals). Learn what kinds of hunting seasons there are — kinds of weapon, time of year, restrictions (what animals cannot be hunted). If you can, find information both in support of and against hunting.

For more projects, go to our website, www.NuggetPress.com

GLOSSARY

Animalia: One of the three broad divisions or kingdoms of natural objects: animal, vegetable and mineral. (There are also *fungi, protista, bacteria* and *monera*).

Bird: Any of the class *Aves* of warm-blooded, egg-laying, feathered vertebrates with forelimbs modified to form wings.

Boreal: Of or pertaining to the forest areas of the northern North Temperate Zone, dominated by coniferous trees such as spruce, fir, and pine.

Carnivore: Any of various predatory, flesh-eating mammals of the order *Carnivora*, including dogs, cats, bears, weasels, hyenas, and raccoons.

Cat: Any the carnivorous mammals of the family *Felidae*, including the lion, tiger, leopard, lynx and mountain lion, as well as domesticated cats.

Class: *Biology:* A taxonomic category ranking below a phylum or division and above an order. [Fish, amphibians, reptiles, birds and mammals are the five classes of vertebrate animals].

Cloven: Having split hoofs, as in cattle or javelina.

Creek: A small stream, often a shallow or intermittent tributary to a river.
Crepuscular: Appearing active in the twilight.

Cud: The portion of food that a ruminant returns from the first stomach to chew a second time.

Deciduous: Shedding or losing foliage at the end of the growing season: *deciduous trees.*

Detrivore, Detritivore: An organism that uses organic waste as a food source, as certain insects do, *e.g.* termites.

Diurnal: Occurring or active during the daytime rather than at night: *diurnal animals.*

Ectotherm: An organism that regulates its body temperature largely by exchanging heat with its surroundings, cold-blooded.

Evergreen: A tree, scrub, or plant having foliage that persists and remains green throughout the year.

Family: *Biology:* A taxonomic category of related organisms ranking below an order and above a genus.

Fauna: The animals of a given region, considered as a whole.

Flora: The plants of a given region, considered as a whole.

Genus: *Biology:* A taxonomic category ranking below a family and above a species and generally consisting of a group of species exhibiting similar characteristics. The genus name is used, often followed by a Latin adjective, to form the name of the species. [e.g., a rattlesnake is a member of the genus *Crotalus cerberus. Crotalus* defines the genus; *cerberus* names the species.]

Herbivore: An animal that feeds chiefly on plants.

Herpetology: Dealing with reptiles and amphibians.

Hibernate: To pass the winter in a dormant or torpid state.

Invertebrate: Lacking a spinal column, including insects and mollusks.

Kingdom: One of the three main divisions (animal, vegetable, and mineral) into which natural organisms and objects are classified. [e.g., Animal Kingdom].

Mammal: Any of various warm-blooded vertebrate animals of the class *Mammalia,* including humans, characterized by a covering of hair on the skin and, in the female, milk-producing mammary glands for nourishing the young.

Monsoon: A wind from the south or southwest that brings heavy rainfall.

Nocturnal: *Zoology:* most active at night: *nocturnal animals.*

Omnivorous: Eating both animal and vegetable foods.

Order: *Biology:* A taxonomic category of organisms ranking above a family and below a class. All animals are in either the carnivore, herbivore, or omnivore order.

Peccary: Any of several piglike hoofed mammals of the family *Tayassuidae,* found in North, Central, and South America and having long, dark, dense bristles.

Phylum: A primary division of a kingdom, as of the animal kingdom, ranking next above a class in size. Most animals are in either the vertebrate or invertebrate (with or without a spinal column) phylum.

Pit Viper: Any of various venomous snakes of the family *Crotalidae,* such as a copperhead, rattlesnake, or fer-de-lance, characterized by a small heat-sensitive pit below each eye.

Predator: An organism that lives by preying on other organisms.

Prey (noun): An animal hunted or caught for food; quarry.

Quarter Horse: A member of the *Equus cabalus* species, usually bred with one fourth Arabian horse, for speed. Common domesticated horse in America.

Retractable: Able to draw back [as the claws of an animal].

Riparian: Of or relating to the bank of a river or other body of water.

Rodent: Any of various mammals of the order *Rodentia,* such as a mouse, rat, squirrel, or beaver, characterized by large incisors adapted for gnawing or nibbling.

Scavenger: An animal or other organism that feeds on dead organic matter; or a person who searches through and collects items from discarded material.

Species: *Biology:* A fundamental category of taxonomic classification, ranking below a genus or subgenus and consisting of related organisms capable of interbreeding. [e.g. all dogs — *canis familiaris* — can interbreed.]

Taxonomy: A way of organizing and categorizing all forms of life.

Ungulate: A mammal with hooves such as horses, rhinoceros, tapir, cattle, pig, giraffe and deer.

Venom: A poisonous secretion of an animal, such as a snake, spider, or scorpion, usually transmitted by a bite or sting.

Venomous: Secreting and transmitting venom; *a venomous snake.*

Vertebrate: Having a backbone or spinal column. Vertebrates are a primary division of the phylum *Chordata* that includes the fishes, amphibians, reptiles, birds and mammals, all of which are characterized by a segmented spinal column and a distinct well-differentiated head.

BRIEF DESCRIPTIONS

These brief descriptions will help the reader learn more about the animals in these stories including their general geographical habitat and some primary features. The descriptions are not intended to be scientifically exhaustive. They are listed below in order of appearance.

ARIZONA BLACK RATTLESNAKE (*Crotalus Cerberus*): Venomous snake, about three-four feet in length, primarily dark gray or black, often with rows of scales in white, yellow or orange across the back. They are carnivorous, preying on amphibians, birds and their eggs, lizards, small mammals. Adults can change color, and snakes care for their young for up to two weeks. They live primarily in the mountain ranges of Arizona.

THE HUMAN FAMILY (*Homo sapiens*): A species of highly intelligent primates in the same family as chimpanzees, gorillas and orangutans. Humans have erect posture, manual dexterity, heavy tool use, complex language use, organized societies. They use systems of symbolic communication such as speech. They have an increasing population that is causing a decrease in the populations of other species.

RED-TAILED HAWK (*Búteo jamaicénsis*): A subfamily of the *accipitridai*, the red-tailed are soaring hawks that circle overhead and drop on prey in a steep dive. They nest in woodlands and hunt in open spaces. They are a family common across the United States, have a broad tail, often perch on poles or treetops. They prey on rabbits and rodents. The call is a high screech.

PET DOG (*Canis lupus familiaris*): Domesticated mammal, not a naturally wild animal. Originally bred from wolves over 15,000 years ago. Dogs are usually playful, friendly, and loyal, and listen to humans. Carnivorous, many breeds work for humans. The dog in *A Rattler's Tale* is a mixed breed Queensland heeler, born in the Navajo Nation. Most Navajo dogs are used for herding cattle or sheep, and thus "heeler" is a common description.

STRIPED SKUNK (*Mephitis mephitis*): Common in Canada, the U.S., and Mexico, the common skunk is omnivorous and polygamous. Its only natural predators are birds of prey, like the hawk. The skunk has musk-filled scent glands to ward off predators. There is an Arizona skunk subspecies with a shorter tail, a smaller skull, and the white stripe is particularly broad on the back and tail. Skunks usually go through threat behaviors before spraying.

GREAT-TAILED GRACKLE (*Quísalus mexicánus*): Common in southwestern towns, mesquite and arid farmlands, especially Texas and southeast New Mexico. Its very long slender V-shaped tail widens at the end. The male has unbarred purple iridescent feathers. The song is of stick-breaking noises, whistles, and rattles.

BLACK-TAILED JACKRABBIT, or AMERICAN DESERT HARE (*Lepus californicus*): One of the largest North American hares, it is found at elevations from sea level up to 10,000 feet altitude, occupying mixed shrub-grassland terrain. Its diet is mostly shrubs, small trees and grasses. It does not migrate or hibernate during winter. It is prey for numerous raptors and carnivorous animals such as hawks and mountain lions.

AMERICAN BLACK BEAR (*Ursus Americanus*): The smallest of the bears, and the most common, especially in Canada, the Northwest, Northeast, and Rocky Mountain region, the American black bear lives in largely forested areas. He is omnivorous, able to eat meats and berries. Sometimes attracted to humans because of food.

WESTERN BLUEBIRD (*Siália mexicána*): Fairly common, with a blue back and blue throat, pinkish/rusty breast, the female has more gray tones. Its usual song is a three-fold or double whistle. The Western bluebird is common in the Southwest north through California.

AMERICAN QUARTER HORSE (*Equus ferus caballus*): An American breed, especially known for sprinting short distances and quick maneuvers such as cutting and barrel racing. The horse has evolved from a smaller multi-toed horse to the modern large single-toed (hoofed) animal. Common domesticated species.

RACCOON (*Procyon lotor*): A medium sized mammal common in North America, with a grayish coat. The raccoon has extremely dexterous front paws, a facial mask and a ringed tail. It can remember solutions to tasks for at least three years. It is nocturnal and omnivorous, with a habitat in deciduous and mixed forests, from mountainous areas to coastal marshes.

FIELD MOUSE, aka VOLE (*Apodemus sylvaticus*): A rodent, the vole/field mouse is a relative of lemmings and hamsters, with a stout body and short hairy tail. There are about one hundred fifty-five vole species. One couple mating can produce about one hundred voles/mice per year. They are generally herbivores and are prey to snakes, birds of prey, and other carnivorous and omnivorous mammals.

JAVELINA aka COLLARED PECCARY (*pecari tajacu*): The peccary is a medium-sized mammal. It resembles a pig, has a snout ending in a cartilaginous disc. It is omnivorous, will eat insects and grubs, but prefers roots, grasses, fruit and cacti. Javelina run in groups or herds called squadrons. They rub their tusks together to make an odor that warns of predators and can find and recognize each other by strong odors.

WHITE TAILED DEER (*Odocoileus Virginianus*): A larger mammal, native to and common throughout North America; lives in a habitat of mixed deciduous riparian corridors. The deer is a hoofed ruminant; a portion of food that a ruminant eats, returns from the first stomach to be chewed a second time. It is a cloven-hoofed quadruped.

MOUNTAIN LION and COUGAR (*Puma concilor*): Medium to large size mammal, native to the Americas, widespread, very adaptable, the second largest cat after the jaguar, closely related to the domestic cat. He is an ambush predator, with primary prey being deer or bears. The habitat is rocky, dense underbrush. He avoids humans.

RINGTAIL (*Bassariscus astutus*): A mammal of the raccoon family, the ringtail is native to the arid regions of North America, such as Arizona. Brown, with a black-and white ringed tail, it is omnivorous, eating birds, rats, mice, snakes, berries and fruits. It is nocturnal, with agile paws and semi-retractable claws well-adapted for climbing. It is prey to foxes, coyotes, raccoons, hawks, owls, and mountain lions. It is adept at avoiding predators and has the ability to excrete musk when startled or threatened. There is a subspecies in Arizona: *Bassariscus astutus arizonensis*.

TAXONOMY CHART

Here is a sample portion of a Taxonomy Chart for four animals in *A Rattler's Tale*. For more categories and more animals check out the full chart at www.NuggetPress.com

TAXONOMY CHART OF ANIMALS IN *A RATTLER'S TALE*

	Rattler	Red-Tailed Hawk	Black Bear	Mountain Lion
Kingdom	Animalia	Animalia	Animalia	Animalia
Phylum	Chordata	Chordata	Chordata	Chordata
Class	Reptilia	Aves	Mammalia	Mammalia
Order	Squamata	Accipitriformes	Carnivora	Carnivora
Family	Viperidae	Accipitridae	Ursidae	Felidae
Genus	Crotalus	Buteo	Ursus	Puma
Species	C.cerberus	B.Jamaicensus	U.americanus	P.concolor

RESOURCES FOR THE CURIOUS

Resources abound to learn even more about the animals who were given a small showcase in *A Rattler's Tale.*

Websites

The Arizona Sonora Desert Museum www.desertmuseum.org

The U.S. Forest Service, U.S. Department of Agriculture www.fs.usda.gov

Arizona Fish and Game Department on raptors, javelina, mountain lions, snakes and more www.azgfd.gov

Phoenix Herpetological Society and Sanctuary on amphibians and reptiles www.phoenixherp.com

U.S. Fish and Wildlife Department www.fws.gov

You will find similar resources in your own state or with your local wildlife museums and sanctuaries.

Books and Magazines

National Parks, The Magazine of the National Parks Conservation Association, describes many animals that inhabit National Parks and that live outside the parks as well.

Nature Conservancy magazine.

Birds

The Sibley Guide to Birds, 2nd Ed., David A. Sibley, Penguin Random House, 2014.

Sibley Birds West: Field Guide to Birds of Western North America, 2nd. Ed., David A. Sibley, Alfred A. Knopf, Inc., 2016.

Sibley Field Guide to Birds of Eastern North America, 2nd Ed., David A. Sibley, Knopf Publishing Group, 2016.

The Genius of Birds, Jennifer Ackerman, Penguin Books, 2017.

H is for Hawk, Helen Macdonald, Grove Press, 2014.

Snakes

Snake: The Essential Visual Guide, Smithsonian Books, Dorley Kindersley Publishing, Inc., 2016.

Mammals

Peterson Field Guide to Mammals of North America, 4th Ed., Fiona Reid, Houghton Mifflen Harcourt Publishing Co., 2006.

National Geographic Book of Mammals, National Geographic Society, National Geographic Kids, 1998.

This is just a starter list. Feel free to explore further as your interest takes you.

ACKNOWLEDGEMENTS

My parents were my first teachers, providing our family with a pet dog and access to the tidal marshes of southern Long Island, where small mammals and wildfowl lived and thrived in abundance. Summer camps on a lake in western Maine, with many hikes to the White Mountains of New Hampshire, offered more exposure to the wild. Even though New York City did not provide a lot of wildlife, many weekend hikes with the Appalachian Mountain Club allowed me to meet my first deer and rattlesnake.

Upon arrival in Arizona in 1975, I met and married the man who introduced me to the cabin in the National Forest, which was the home base for these vignettes. It has been a privilege to observe from the safety of a cabin porch — and beyond.

The first people to support this writing project were Richard and Marilyn Mueller, who enthusiastically endorsed the snake as the story-teller. Everyone with whom I have compared writing notes has helped in forming this style along with content, but all blunders are my own.

I give special thanks to both our children, who as youngsters enjoyed our many adventures in the forest. As adults, they each lived in that cabin for a time, clearing dead ponderosa after the bark beetle infestation in the early 2000s and describing some sightings that made their way into *"A Rattler's Tale."*

Finally, deep thanks to Vance, who kept insisting we go back again and again. I wouldn't have missed it for the world.

ABOUT THE AUTHOR

Nancy Hicks Marshall grew up near the tidal marshes of southern Long Island, New York. She attended summer camp on a lake in western Maine for several years. When living in New York City, she hiked in New York and New England. She moved to Arizona in 1975 and has frequently visited the National Forests in Yavapai and Coconino Counties. She and her husband and children often visited their cabin in the Prescott National Forest, a location where these stories are based.

Ms. Marshall's professional career includes time as a public school teacher (K-12), Project Coordinator of affordable housing, Executive Director of the Arizona Civil Liberties Union, and work as an attorney in the Juvenile Court. She has authored several books including fiction, non-fiction, and embellished fact. She lives in Arizona with her husband and their dog, Chelly.

ABOUT THE ARTIST

Lauren Sarantopulos is a wildlife artist who has been painting and drawing since she was ten. Based out of Flagstaff, AZ, Lauren also works as a fisheries biologist, helping to conserve native fish species in the Grand Canyon. She hopes that her passion for and knowledge of the environment and the arts will help to bring people closer to nature and draw attention to pressing issues such as endangered species loss and wildlife conservation.

CPSIA information can be obtained
at www.ICGtesting.com
Printed in the USA
LVHW101638011121
702139LV00005B/290

9 780982 825907